The Essential Electric Pie-Maker Cookbook

Table of Contents

Introduction

For many of us, it has always been a struggle to try to provide our families with good, nutritious food, while maintaining a busy lifestyle. This used to m3ean a lot of pre-packaged foods, and take-out items. Places like Kentucky Fried Chicken, McDonald's and other fast-food places, have built multi-million dollar empires by catering to the working masses. And, for the most part, they do a fine job of providing what the customer wants, or thing they want. But fast food restaurants are just as much victims of the Big Food Industry as you and I. The ingredients they use contain the same additives, food colorings, fillers and preservatives as the things we buy at the grocery store.

Even the ones of us who avoided the fast food circus still had to deal with all of these additives even in our frozen foods. When I was growing up, one of our favorite things to eat were pot pies. Those delicious round little tarts were just bursting with flavors of chicken, beef, turkey and vegetables, in a wonderful gravy, and contained in a great pie crust. But, they also contained (and still do) msg, preservatives, and a lot of other things that are better avoided when possible. And, you were limited to those three flavors.

Fast-forward to the 21st century. Thanks to technology, we have all kinds of appliances available to make our life easier. Now, anyone can prepare world-class dishes with a minimum of fuss. You don't have to be a Certified Chef to provide your family with gourmet-quality chow. And one of the neatest of the kitchen gadgets is the electronic pie-maker.

Modern Electronic Pie Makers are sold by many companies, like Nostalgia Electronics, Breville, Sunbeam, Emeril, Wolfgang Puck, and more. Regardless of who sells them, they all work about the same. They are based on the principle of a waffle iron. Basically, all you have to do is insert a bottom pie crust cut to the correct size, load it with your filling, top it with another crust, close the lid, and when it is done, remove the pies and chow-down. You can now have homemade pot pies, and tarts anytime you want, with ingredients you select yourself. The filling can be made from anything you can imagine. Breakfast, lunch and dinner can be a whole new proposition, with one of these little gadgets on your kitchen shelf.

In the following chapters, I'll be expanding on pies, and the machines, as well as providing you with several dozen great recipe ideas. If you have ever wanted to learn about personal pies, you've come to the right place.

Part 1 - The Basics

Chapter 1-Exactly What Is A Pie?

In the modern world, a pie is a baked dish consisting of a pastry crust stuffed with various fillings, Pies are divided into types according to their fillings and crusts. *Savory pies* usually contain meat and/or vegetables and are not sweet, but used as a main dish. This would include things like chicken pie, British meat pies, and so on. *Sweet pies* contain fruit, puddings or other dessert items and are served as a compliment to the main meal. A *filled pie* has a bottom crust with the filling on top. A *cobbler* has the filling at the bottom, and the crust on top. A *two-crust pie* is a filled pie with a top crust. A *tart* is a personal-sized pie, usually two crust, or otherwise sealed. There are other specialty pies as well, such as *fried pies, turnovers, calazones, empanadas,* and *strombolis,* These are beyond the scope of this book, so we will be concentrating on filled, and two-crust pies that are suitable for an electronic pie maker.

We believe the first flour appeared around 9000 BC, during the Neolithic, or New Stone Age period, soon after the advent of agriculture. In Ancient Egypt, stone grinding wheels were used to grind oats, rye, barley and wheat. The first pastries were honey wrapped in a mixture of ground oats, barley and wheat flour. The recipe for this was found on the tomb walls of Ramses II in the Valley of Kings. Cultural exchange helped the idea to spread, and a recipe for chicken pie was found in an excavation site in Sumer dating from around 2000 BC. These first pie crusts were just flour and water, used as just a container for the filling. They were very hard, and mostly inedible, unless you were really hungry.

The Greeks got a hold of the recipes, and added some fat to the flour/water mixture, and the first true pastry was born. It wasn't long before the Romans began experimenting with the new pastry, and one of their favorites was a pie known as *Placenta,* which is still around today, luckily under the more appetizing name of cheesecake. In the 1st Century AD, the Romans published a cookbook called the *Apicus*, probably the worlds first real cookbook. It contained many recipes involving pastries and pies. As the Roman Empire spread, so did their culinary knowledge, and pies soon were being baked all over Europe. A few were sweet pies, but the popular taste was for meat and vegetable based pies.

After the fall of the Roman Empire, and throughout the Dark Ages, pies became an important staple. Pies were portable, and helped to preserve food on long journeys. By medieval times, pies were a major part of the European diet. But cooks during the Middle Ages had very limited resources. Ovens were expensive to build and maintain. Many times, pies were cooked over open fires, and hearths. Limited resources also meant that fillings had to be made from whatever was available, so songbird pies were very commonplace, hence the rhyme, *"Four and twenty blackbirds baked in a pie"*. During the Renaissance, it became popular among royal courts to have cold pies made with live bird and other animals, and in at least one case, a midget, so that they could fly, crawl, or run away when the pie was cut. Thankfully, this was a short-lived trend.

It's been said that nothing is as American as apple pie, but like most American customs, apple pie had its' beginnings in England. As early as the 1500s, unsweetened apples were baked in an inedible crust, and these became quite popular. Sweet pies didn't really become popular until the 20th century. Cookbooks from the 1700s only listed 3 types of sweet pies. In the 1800s, most cookbooks only listed 8 types of sweet pie, mostly fruit. By the mid- 1900s, cookbooks were describing more than 65 styles of sweet pies. So, not to bust anyone's bubble, but the tradition of pumpkin, sweet potato, and pecan pies for Thanksgiving as nothing to do with the Pilgrims. It is a modern tradition added to the holiday. When the pilgrims landed at Plymouth Rock, they had neither the ingredients, nor the desire to bake any pies, and Native American weren't real big on pies themselves.

Pies as we know them today really started to get popular in the mid 1800s, and the introduction of modern conveniences like commercial flour, canned fruits and meats, canned milk, and Crisco helped a lot by making it much easier and quicker to bake pies, with more consistent results. Today, there are few kitchens that do not have some of the ingredients for making pies available at all times. Small meat, veggie and gravy-filled pies known as 'Pot Pies" are especially popular. So much so that some appliance manufacturers have even made a special gadget just to make them in....which is the subject of this book.

Enjoy.

Chapter 2-Getting To Know Your Pie Maker

Your pie-maker came with a manual, and if it became lost, copies can be easily downloaded at www.wpcookware.com/instructions/BPM00020.pdf , so I won't be going into safety precautions, specifications, and other things that are in the manual. Likewise, I won't be providing any warranty information, either. You should have all of that already. I will say that these little gadgets are well-made, and I have had no problems with them, even after dropping them several times (*but this is not recommended....just take my word for it....*).

Here are some tips that will help your pie-maker to work better, and last longer:

- Always keep your pie-maker as clean as possible, but never immerse it completely in water. Keep water away from the electrical parts as much as possible. If you do accidentally get those parts wet, wipe off as much water as possible, allow it to dry completely before plugging it in.

- Never use metal utensils, or abrasive cleaning agents, scouring pads, etc. The exception is the little metal fork supplied with your unit. It is just to life the edge of the crust up so you can get the plastic spatula under it. It never makes contact with any of the non-stick surfaces. If you need to really scrub the insides, use a non-metal brush, or plastic scrubbies. Never use Scotchbrite pads or steel wool (*and yes, SOS pads are also metal, so don't use these either*). These will destroy the non-stick coating, effectively ruining your appliance. You could try to use non-stick cooking spray if that happens, but it's been my experience that it will never work the same again. It's better just to take care of the unit from the first.

- Don't touch any of the electrical parts, connections, etc...while the unit is on. It can burn you. Allow the unit to cool-down completely before trying to clean it, so as not to cause any warping of the metal parts.

- I always wipe a little olive, or vegetable oil on the cooking surfaces before using the pie-maker, because it browns the bottom crust better, and makes it a little easier to lift the edge of the crust without damaging the pies, when they are done.

- Avoid using commercial non-stick sprays. They all leave a sticky residue that is hard to clean off. You won't need to use them anyway, if you take care of your pie-maker.

- When making anything that rises, like muffins, biscuits, don't fill the compartments more than 2/3rds full, or it will make a mess (...*ever overfill a waffle-iron? This will do the same thing....*)

- The green light is not a timer, and does not mean the pies are ready. It just means the heating element is at the correct temperature. Your unit will cycle between the red and green lights several times during the baking process. It just means the unit maintaining the correct temperature. Always use a kitchen timer, stopwatch, sand-dial, sun-dial, or whatever...to time the baking process. These pie-makers work pretty much just like an electric waffle iron.

- It's a good idea to unplug the unit before opening the lid, and removing the pies, just for a little extra safety. If the pies need more time, you can always just close the lid and plug it back in. It won't hurt the pies at all.

- Always use the dough-cutters that came with your unit. They make perfect-sized pie crusts, every time. If you have to use store-bought crusts, you can get two crusts from each one, for a total of 4 crusts...two bottoms, and two tops (...*but I highly recommend practicing a lot and learning how to make your own crusts...your pies will be a lot better...I have included a chapter on crusts, coming up...)*

- When putting the bottom crust in the pie-maker, don't use the method described in the manual. It can result in a mess, and a ruined pie. They recommend laying the bottom over the compartment, and ladling the filling in, and letting the weight of the filling push the crust down. This problem is that the crust will not always go down evenly, and once it is filled, there is nothing you can do to fix it without tearing up the crust. Draping the crust over your fingers and easing the crust in is a better method, unless you have long fingernails. Long fingernails can tear the crust. I play finger-style guitar, so I keep the first three fingernails on my right hand a little long, so I have t be careful to use my left hand to do load crusts. Another solution is to use the back of a small ladle to drape the crust over, and ease it in.

- If disaster happens (*and it will, sometimes, no matter how careful you are...,* and you tear the crust after it is in the unit, all is not necessarily lost. In most cases, it is possible to make a 'patch' from the extra dough, and repair the crust. Just press the 'patch' gently over the tear and blend the edges carefully. If you tear the crust before putting it in the pie-maker, just toss it back into the dough and roll it out again. Then cut a new crust, and be more careful this time.

If you follow these tips, your pie-maker should last a very long time, and you will enjoy using it a lot more.

Part 2 - Crusts

Chapter 1 - It's All In The Crust

You can, of course, simply use store bought pie crusts, and just cut them to size, but the whole idea behind getting your pie-maker was so you could make your own pies, the way you want them. So, why not learn to make the crusts, too? Then, you have complete control over the entire process.

If there is anything that really terrifies a lot of would-be bakers, it is having to make pie crusts. For a lot of novice cooks, pie crusts are a roll of the dice. Sometimes they come out OK, and other times you wind up with a chewy, leathery mess. And they have no idea what went wrong because they used the same recipe. If you are one of these unfortunates, don't fret. You are not alone.

There are those that somehow instinctively grasp the science of pie crusts, without even being aware of it. This has often been referred to as "art", and "talent", and these lucky people are in high demand in restaurants and commercial kitchens all over the world. Pie and Pastry chefs usually earn top-dollar, and are more than worth it. However, it really is just a matter of science, and just about anyone can learn how to make world-class pie crusts, with a little practice.

Before you start mixing ingredients, it helps to have an idea of what you want the finished product to be like. As a rule, what we are looking for is a crust that is durable enough not to get soggy from the filling, but tender enough to so that it flakes in your mouth with delicious, buttery flavor and texture, and not crumbly like a cracker. We do not want a crust that is chewy, doughy, tough, or hard.

The basic recipe for pie crust sounds deceptively simple. It's just four ingredients: flour, fat, salt, and water. Easy, right? Well... yes, and no. It's more about how the ingredients go together, than the actual ingredients themselves. Of course, there are subtle differences that can be achieved by using different flours, different fats, and liquids, but these four ingredients are all you need.

The basic technique is to add salt, and cut the fat into the flour, then add the liquid a little at a time until it just forms a ball. Then all you have to do is roll it out and cut it to shape. But there is a lot more to it than that. You need to understand what is happening at each stage.

Chapter 2 - Flour Power

The salt is just for flavor, so we don't have to worry much about that. Just don't over do it. But when we cut the fat into the flour, several things are happening here. First, when you add water to flour, it starts to form gluten, which is what makes bread possible. And the more you manipulate the dough, the more gluten forms. But we don't want a bready crust, so we want to limit this as much as possible. One way is to use low-gluten flours, also called 'soft' flour. Pastry flours work very well. Try to avoid using 'hard' varieties of flour. These are better suited for making bread and pasta. You want to keep the gluten content below 11% as much as possible. All Purpose flour can be used, which has a gluten content of around 12%, but I advise against using Self-Rising flours. I know there are those that swear by using Self-Rising flour in pie crusts, but it's been my experience that the crusts come out tasting and feeling more like a thin biscuit, rather than a pie crust...probably OK if you're making a chicken or meat pie, but otherwise.....not for me... If you insist on using Self-Rising flour, then omit the salt, because Self-Rising flour has plenty of salt already in it, as well as some baking soda., which really isn't desirable in a pie crust.

Chapter 3 - A Short Lecture On Texture.....

Cutting the fat into the flour causes the little globs of fat to become coated with flour, which absorbs some of the liquid from the fat. Fats can contain anywhere from 7% to 15% water, depending on what kind you use, and how it was rendered. Once the flour absorbs a little or the water from the fat, it forms a pasty boundary layer on the outside of the glob that prevents further moistening. So, when you roll the dough out, you get layers of flour and gluten, alternating with layers of fat, with a very thin boundary between each layer. This is known as 'stratifying', similar to what you see when a road it cut through a hill, with each layer of rock plainly visible. This what makes a flaky pie crust. The trick is that the fat and flour have to be in the right proportions. Too little fat, and you wind up with a crumbly cracker for a crust. Too much and you wind up with a tough, chewy mess. Also, you don't want to cut the fat/flour mixture too fine. This will also make the crust crumbly, rather than flaky.

If you mess up and get the texture too fine, you can simply cut in a little more flour and fat. Just be careful not to overwork the dough.

Chapter 4 - Fat Is Where It's At....

This is one of the most hotly debated issues in the cooking world: whether to use butter, lard or shortening in your pie crusts. If you are thinking, *"Why didn't he mention margarine?"*, then you need to read no further. Sell your machine, and stick to buying those frozen pies at the store. Margarine will not work at all, and is an abomination from a culinary point of view, suitable only for greasing pans and cooking eggs in. I suppose you could use it for sautéing, if nothing else is available...Using margarine will do nothing but make a crumbly, soft mess, which is why it's not used in cookies, either, (*not good ones, anyway...*).

Each type of fat has it's good and bad points. And everyone has their favorite, which they defend viciously. Here is a run-down of each type, and it's good and bad points:

- **Butter**: *Pros*-outstanding flavor and makes nice flaky layers. *Cons*-Butter melts at a very low temperature (lower than body temperature), so it is very difficult to work with. It also has more water than any other fat (15%-17%), which means it causes more gluten to form. This can make your crust leathery and tough if you are not very careful. Butter should be frozen before cutting it into the flour.

- **Lard** (my favorite): *Pros*-has a wide workable temperature range, and is not as soft as either butter, or shortening at these levels. Very forgiving, and makes outstanding light, flaky crusts. *Cons*-It can be difficult to find good lard, unless you render your own. Some store-bought lard (the cheaper brands) have a strongish odor of pork, which you don't want in your crusts. Stick to the better name brands, or better yet, get your lard from a butcher shop, or meat market that renders their own. Always keep your lard in a cool (< 80ºF) place, or it may turn rancid rather quickly. For making pie crusts, it is best to chill the lard for an hour or two in the refrigerator before using it.

- **Shortening**: *Pros-* cheap and easy to work with. Makes tender crusts. *Cons*: has no flavor at all. Also has a low melting point, like butter. This makes it easy to overwork the dough, making it crumbly instead of flaky.

Whichever fat you decide to use, here are a few tips to make your crusts turn out better:

- Keep your ingredients as cold as possible while making the crust. Use ice water, frozen butter, and chilled lard. It they start to warm up, then put them back in the fridge for a few minutes, then continue after they have re-chilled..

- If you don't have a digital kitchen scale, the go get one. This is an essential kitchen tool. Measure your flour by weight, not volume. Flour volume can vary as much as 50% depending on how tightly it is packed, and how fine it was ground. A cup of flour averages 5 ounces (142 grams) of flour. 5 ounces is 5 ounces no matter how tightly it is packed.

- If you don't have a food processor, get one. Another essential kitchen tool. Nothing is better for cutting fat into flour evenly. Just operate it in quick pulses until the dough just starts to ball up, and your crusts will be great. Of course, it is possible to use a spoon, or even your hands, if you work quickly enough, but it is to cut the fat into the flour fast enough to keep the fat from reaching it's melting point, especially with shortening and butter. And if you use your hands, the heat from your hands speeds up the melting process. Trust me on this one...a food processor is the way to go on this...

- After cutting the fat and flour, it's time to add the water (*I know some people like to use milk, but don't....it makes the crust crumblier...*). But resist the temptation to add the ice water directly to the dough in the food processor. It will over-process the dough and make the crust crumbly instead of flaky. Remove the dough to another bowl and work the water into it slowly with a rubber (silicon) spatula. Don't muse your hands. The heat from your hands will cause the fat to start melting, and ruin your crust.

- After adding the water, make the dough into a ball, place it in a zip-lock baggie, or wrap it in plastic wrap, and chill it in the fridge for at least 30 minutes before rolling it out. This allows the dough to 'rest' as well as keep the fat cold. It really makes a big difference.

- Small, tapered French-style rolling pins work better than the large, baseball-bats with handles that are common in most kitchens. Hang grandma's 3' solid oak rolling pin on the wall for use in home and kitchen defense against intruders, and get a small, light French-style rolling pin. We're trying to gently coax our dough into a nice, light, thin layer...not beat it into submission. A small rolling pin gives you much more control over what you are doing.

Keeping these tips in mind, here are a few of the best pie crust recipes, starting with my favorite. They should make more than enough dough for four mini-crusts (2 tops and 2 bottoms).

Basic Pie Crust

10 oz. (2 cups) soft white flour

* 2/3 cup chilled lard

¼ cup ice-water

1 tsp salt

Sift four and salt together 3 times. Transfer flour/salt to your food processor. Add lard and pulse until the mixture has the appearance of pea-gravel. Don't over-do it.

Transfer the mix to a mixing bowl and working quickly, add ice-water a teaspoon at a time, blending with a spatula, until the dough just starts to form a ball. Place the ball into a baggie and chill in the fridge for at least 30 minutes. The dough can stay in the fridge for as long as 12 hours with no harm.

When ready to make the crusts, pinch off golf ball-sized pieces of dough and roll into a smaller ball. Return the rest of the dough to the fridge until you are ready to make the other crusts, so it will stay cold.

Flour your working space, your hands, and the rolling pin, but not too much, or it make make the dough tough.

Starting from the center, roll the dough out, and rotate ¼ or a turn each time. Once you have gone all the way around, flip the dough over and repeat. Keep doing this until the desired size and thickness is achieved.

Repeat this process until all of your crusts are made. If you want to make them up ahead of time, they can be stacked between layers of wax, or parchment paper and chilled, or even frozen until ready to use.

* Note-This recipe can also be used with butter, or shortening, all in the same proportions.

Part 3 – Recipes

Dessert Pies

Apple Pie

8 cups diced, peeled assorted baking apples

2 Tbs lemon juice

3/4 cup white sugar

1/4 cup brown sugar

1/4 cup all-purpose flour

1 tsp ground cinnamon

1/4 tsp ground nutmeg

2 Tbs butter

1 egg yolk

1 Tbs milk

Pie crusts for 8 mini-pies

In a large bowl, toss the diced apples with lemon juice.

Combine sugars, flour, cinnamon and nutmeg; add to apples and toss well to coat.

Place bottom crust in pie-maker. Load filing.

Place second crust on top of pie filling, cut slits in top of crust to vent.

Bake for 15 minutes or until crust is golden brown

Makes 8 mini pies

Banana Pie

4 ripe bananas, sliced

1/4 cup cornstarch

1 cup sugar

1/4 tsp salt

3 cups milk

4 egg yolks, beaten

3 Tbs butter

1 1/2 tsp vanilla

8 baked mini-pie crusts

In a medium saucepan combine sugar, cornstarch, and salt; gradually stir in milk.

Cook and stir over medium heat till thickened.

Reduce heat, cook and stir 2 minutes more. Remove from heat.

Separate egg whites; discard. Beat egg yolks slightly.

Gradually stir 1 cup of the hot mixture into the egg yolks. Return egg mixture to saucepan; bring to a gentle boil. Cook and stir an additional 2 minutes.

Remove from heat. Stir in the vanilla, butter, and three of the sliced bananas.\

Place bottom crust in pie-maker

Pour filling in crust.

Close the lid and bake for 12 to 15 minutes. Remove from pie maker, cool.

Repeat until all filling and crusts are used.

Prepare the topping by beating the whipping cream until soft peaks form. Add the sugar and beat until stiff peaks form.

Place topping onto the banana filling, chill for 1-2 hours before serving

Serves 8

Black Bottom Pie

1/2 cup sugar
1 Tbs cornstarch
2 cups milk, scalded
4 egg yolks, beaten
1 tsp vanilla
6 oz package chocolate chips
1/4 oz envelope unflavored gelatin
1/4 cup cold water
4 egg whites
1/2 cup sugar
8 crusts, pre-cooked

Place two crusts in pie-maker and bake until golden brown. Remove and repeat for all the crusts.

Combine 1/2 cup sugar and cornstarch in the top of a double boiler.

Slowly add scalded milk to beaten egg yolks; stir into sugar mixture.

Cook and stir in top of double boiler over hot, but not boiling, water until custard coats spoon.

Remove from heat and add vanilla to 1 cup of the custard.

Add the chocolate chips and stir until melted.

Pour this mixture into the bottom of the baked and cooled pie shells and chill.

Meanwhile, soften gelatin in cold water and add remaining hot custard. Stir until dissolved. Chill until slightly thick.

Beat egg whites until soft peaks form; beat in 1/2 cup sugar and continue beating until stiff peaks form. Fold in the custard gelatin mixture.

Pile over chocolate layer; chill until set.

Makes 8 pies

Birds Nest Pie

4 -5 medium apples, peeled and diced
2 cups all-purpose flour
1 cup sugar
1 cup buttermilk
1 egg
1 tbsp baking powder

Topping

1/4 cup sugar
1/2 tsp ground cinnamon
1/4 tsp ground nutmeg

Divide apples evenly and set aside.

In a mixing bowl, combine flour, sugar, baking soda, cream of tartar, sour milk, or yogurt, and egg; mix well.

Divide batter and pour over apples.

Bake for 25-30 minutes or until pies are lightly browned and test done.

Immediately invert onto serving plates (so apples are on the top).

Combine all topping ingredients; sprinkle over apples.

Makes about 8 pies

Serve warm.

Blueberry Pie

6 cups fresh blueberries

2 Tbs all-purpose flour

1/2 cup sugar

1/4 tsp ground cinnamon

1/4 tsp ground nutmeg

8 prepared mini pie crust

8 pastry tops

Combine 2 tablespoons flour, sugar, cinnamon and nutmeg together.

Stir in the blueberries.

Spoon blueberry mixture into prepared chilled mini pie crust.

Place top crust on pies and perforate with fork.

Bake for 35 minutes and check

Continue baking for an additional 10 to 20 minutes or until crust is lightly browned and juice begins to bubble through cut-outs in crust.

Serves 8

Chocolate Pie

1 2/3 cups water

1 (14 ounce) can eagle brand sweetened condensed milk

3 Tbs cornstarch

5 Tbs cocoa

3 egg yolks, beaten

2 Tbs butter

1 tsp vanilla

8 baked mini pie shells

Mix water and cornstarch and cocoa until smooth.

Sir in Eagle Brand milk and egg yolks.

Cook until thick in saucepan or microwave.

Stir in 2 tbsp butter.

Add vanilla.

Cool slightly (stirring occasionally).

Pour into baked mini pie shells.

Top with whipped cream after chilling pie.

Peach Pie

6 medium peaches

1 cup sugar

1/3 cup flour

1 tsp lemon juice

pinch salt

8 baked mini pie crust

8 pastry tops

Wash peaches, remove seed, peel and dice.

In a large bowl, combine peaches, sugar, flour, salt and lemon juice.

Pour mixture into a prepared pie crust.

Place the top crust on pie

Cut a few slits in the top of the pie crust to let steam escape.

Close pie maker and bake for 35-45 minutes or until crust is golden

Sprinkle some sugar on the top of the pie crust.

Serve warm or chilled

Main Dish Pies

BBQ and Potato Pie

1 lb ground pork

barbecue sauce, to taste

1 large or 2 medium potatoes

4 oz sharp cheddar cheese

8mini pastry bottoms

8 pastry tops

Brown ground pork in skillet and drain.

BBQ sauce to thoroughly cover all the pork.

Cook and dice potato

Add BBQ and potatoes

Place crust bottom in pie maker

Pour mixture into raw crust and top with shredded cheese.

Place top crusts

Bake until golden brown and serve while hot

Great served with coleslaw and beans

Serves 8

BBQ Chicken Pie

2 cups shredded chicken

1 cup shredded cheese of choice

8 baked mini pie crust

½ cup barbecue sauce

In medium bowl, mix chicken and sauce.

Spoon chicken mixture into crust in pie makers

Top with cheese.

Bake until cheese is golden

Serves 8

Broccoli, Ham and Cheese Pie

8 mini pie crust bottoms and tops

1 ½ cups cubed (1/4 inch) cooked ham

1 ½ cups shredded Swiss cheese

1 cup frozen broccoli florets, thawed and drained

4 eggs

1 cup milk

½ tsp salt

½ tsp dry ground mustard

½ tsp pepper

Place ham, cheese and broccoli into baked pie crusts

Beat eggs and milk with fork until blended

Add remaining ingredients

Place tops on pies

Bake in pie maker until done

Serves 8

Cabbage and Ham Pie

1 1/2 lbs. baked ham, diced

6 russet potatoes, peeled and diced

1 head savoy cabbage, diced

6 Tbsp. flour

5 cups milk

1 cup heavy cream

2/3 cup chopped fresh parsley

14 Tbsp. butter

Salt and freshly ground black pepper

2 scallions, trimmed and finely chopped

Cook potatoes in cold water over medium-high heat until soft

Melt 6 tbsp. of the butter in a medium saucepan over medium heat

Add flour and cook, stirring, for 2 minutes.

Add milk and cook, stirring often, until sauce thickens

Add parsley and salt and pepper to taste and set aside.

Boil cabbage in a medium pot of boiling salted water over high heat until soft and drain.

Drain potatoes and mash until smooth.

Combine potatoes and cabbage

Stir in cream, the remaining 8 tbsp. butter, scallions, and salt and pepper to taste and set aside.

Place ham in bottom of pie maker

Combine cabbage, then sauce, then mashed potatoes, in that order

Bake until bubbling hot and golden on top.

Serves 8

Cheese Burger Pie

1 1/4 lbs extra lean ground beef (pork or turkey)
1/2 cup ketchup
1/2 cup evaporated milk

1/4 cup onion (chopped fine)

1 egg (beaten)
4 slices bread (toasted dry and crumbed)
1/2 tsp salt
1/2 tsp dried oregano

1/4 tsp pepper
1/4 tsp minced garlic
2 unbaked mini pie shells

Cheese For Topping

1 cup sharp cheddar cheese (grated)

2 Tbs Worcestershire sauce

Combine first ten (10) ingredients.

Press meat mixture into unbaked pie shells.

Bake for 50 minutes.

Combine cheese and Worcestershire sauce and spread on top of baked meat pie.

Bake an additional 10 minutes.

Cool 10-15 minutes before serving.

Makes about 8 individual pies

Chicken Pot Pie

1 cup cooked chicken, cut into bite sized pieces

1 2/3 cups frozen vegetables, thawed

1 (10 ounce) can cream of chicken soup

1/2 cup nonfat milk or 1/2 cup milk

1 egg

8 mini pie crust bottoms (baked)

8 mini pie crust tops

Mix chicken, veggies and cream of chicken soup together and spoon into baked crust

Place top crust on pie

Bake until golden brown.

Serves 8

Chorizo Empanadas

1 cup shredded sharp Cheddar cheese

½ cup Mexican chorizo

8 oz cream cheese

1 egg, beaten

1 small onion, chopped

½ red bell pepper, chopped

1 small jalapeño, diced

1 clove garlic, diced

½ tsp cumin

8 baked pie bottoms

8 tops (unbaked)

Cook chorizo in skillet until lightly done and crumble.

Add onions, bell pepper, garlic, and cumin.

Stir and heat until translucent.

Beat the cream cheese in a bowl until smooth.

Stir in the chorizo mixture and Cheddar cheese

Pour into prepared baked pie crust.

Top with crust and bake until golden brown

Serve warm

Serves 8

Chorizo Pie

16 oz ground Mexican chorizo (fresh or dried)

1 can corn, drained

1 can diced tomatoes with jalapeno

1/2 onion diced

1 clove garlic, minced

6 oz Mexican shredded cheese

1 green onion, chopped

Fresh cilantro, chopped

1 diced jalapeno, seeds removed

8 mini pie crust baked

Cook chorizo in skillet until done

Add onion, garlic, green onion, stir until onion is translucent

Add remaining ingredients and scoop into prepared baked crust

Bake until mixture is hot

Dollop with salsa and sour cream or Mexican Creama

Serves 8

Egg can be added for a breakfast pie. Mashed potatoes can be added to make shepherds pie. The combinations are endless. And delicious.

Corn Bread BBQ Pie

Pulled pork or beef from left over roast

1 cup barbecue sauce

½ diced onion

1 cup corn bread mix

Mix pulled meat, bbq sauce, onion and corn bread mix

Pour into pie maker and bake until golden brown

Serves 8

Double Meat Pot Pie

1 1/2 lbs lean ground beef

8 oz ground pork

1/2 cup dried cranberries

2 medium carrots or parsnips, peeled

1 medium russet potato, peeled

1 small onion

1 cup nonfat milk

2 tsp ground allspice

1 tsp salt

1/2 tsp freshly ground pepper

8 mini pie crust and tops (unbaked)

Cut potato, carrots (or parsnips) and onion in food processor in pieces that will fit through the tube. Add vegetables until they're all shredded.

Combine beef, pork, milk and the shredded vegetables in a high-sided skillet or pan.

Cook over medium heat, mashing and stirring with a potato masher, until the meat is dry.

Reduce heat and continue

Stir in cranberries, allspice, salt and pepper.

Place pie crust in pie maker

Scoop filling into the crust

Place top crust

Close and bake until golden brown

Serves 8

Meatloaf and Potato Pie

1-1/2 lbs ground beef

2 eggs

1 cup 2% milk

1-3/4 cups soft bread crumbs

1/2 cup shredded cheddar cheese

1/4 cup chopped onion

1 envelope (7.6 ounces) butter and herb instant mashed potatoes

1 tsp salt

1 tsp prepared mustard

1/2 tsp rubbed sage

1/4 tsp pepper

Combine the first seven ingredients.

Crumble beef over mixture and mix well.

Press onto the bottom and up the sides of the pie maker.

Bake until meat is no longer pink

Meanwhile, prepare mashed potatoes according to package directions and stir in mustard.

Spread potatoes over top.

Sprinkle with cheese.

Bake 3-5 minutes longer or until cheese is melted.

Let stand for 5 minutes before serving

Serves 8

Mexican BBQ Pork Pie

4 to 4 1/2 pounds pork butt

8 mini pie crust and tops(unbaked)

1/4 cup red pepper, diced

1/4 cup green pepper, diced

1 jalapeno, seeded and diced

1/4 cup onion, diced

1/3 cup ketchup

1/3 cup yellow mustard

1/3 cup molasses

1/3 cup brown sugar

1 tbsp hot sauce

1 tbsp oil

Salt and Pepper

Egg wash

Saute peppers and onion in oil until translucent.

Mix ketchup, mustard, molasses, brown sugar, and hot sauce.

Pour over vegetables and stir.

Cook 3-5 minutes in sauce pan.

Season the pork with salt and pepper (rub it in well) and smoke 1-2 hours, basting 2 or 3 times with BBQ sauce.

When done, cool and shred.

Add BBQ sauce.

Add pork to pie crust, apply top crust.

Bake until golden brown

Serves 8

Mexican Lasagna Pie

1 lb lean lean ground beef

1½ cups shredded Cheddar cheese

16 oz cottage cheese, Parmesan or Queso Blanco

16-oz salsa

15½ oz cooked black beans, drained

10 oz bag frozen corn

1 lg carrot, shredded

1 tsp chili powder

1 tsp gr cumin

prepared crust disks, 8 bottom and 8 tops

Cook the meat and carrot in a large skillet over medium-high heat and drain

Add the salsa, black beans, corn, chili powder, and cumin to the skillet and stir until mixed well

Layer meat mixture, cheeses, salsa in pie shells

Place crust tops

Bake in pie maker until golden brown

Dollop sour cream or salsa on top and serve warm

Serves 8

Mexican Meatloaf Pie

1 1/4 lb. ground beef (90% lean)

1 cup finely crushed tortilla chips

1 cup shredded pepper Jack cheese

1 can golden hominy rinsed & drained

1 can diced tomatoes with green chilies, drained

1/2 cup cooked rice

1 envelope onion soup mix

1/4 cup bottled taco sauce

1/4 cup chopped fresh cilantro

2 eggs, lightly beaten (divided)

1 medium fresh jalapeño pepper, seeded & chopped

Combine beef, crushed chips, soup mix, 1/2 cup of taco sauce, one lightly beaten egg, and 1/2 tsp. black pepper.

Press into bottom & sides of pie maker.

Add rice, hominy, tomatoes, cheese, Jalapeño pepper, cilantro & taco sauce & egg.

Spoon into meat shell.

Bake until done

Top with chips, jalapeño & cilantro.

Makes 8 servings.

Pizza Pot Pie

1 (24 oz) jar traditional-style pasta sauce (I use my own home made)

8 oz wagon wheel macaroni

1 (8 oz) package mozzarella cheese, cut into thin slices

8 oz Italian sausage

1 tsp instant minced onion

1/2 tsp oregano

1/2 tsp basil

1/4 tsp ground black pepper

8 mini pie shells

Cook and drain pasta as directed on package.

While pasta is cooking, break apart Italian sausage and cook over medium heat in a large skillet, until done, about 5-7 minutes

Add in onion, oregano, basil and pepper, stir well and drain

Stir cooked sausage, onion, oregano, basil and pepper into pasta sauce in bowl

Add cooked pasta, blend well.

Pour into pie crust

Bake 15 minutes

While hot cover top completely with mozzarella slices.

Great served with garlic bread or garlic sticks and a side salad.

Pork Pot Pie

1/4 lb cooked and shredded pork

16 oz cooked black beans

1 cup shredded cheddar cheese

14 oz diced tomatoes

11 oz corn, drained
1/2 cup freshly chopped cilantro
1 medium onion, chopped

4 cloves garlic, chopped

1 zucchini, diced

1 tbsp olive oil
1 tbsp chili powder

1 tsp ground cumin
1 tsp oregano
1 tsp salt

1/2 tsp coriander
Black pepper to taste

8 baked mini pie crust

Saute onion and garlic until translucent.

Add zucchini, cumin, chili powder and salt.

Stir in tomatoes with juice, beans, corn, cilantro and meat; heat through. Add shredded pork

Place into baked crust

Bake until mixture is hot, sprinkle with cheese and top with sour cream

Serves 8

Roast BBQ Pie

Left over roast, pork or beef

8 mini pie shell bottoms (baked) and 8 tops

1 cup shredded cheese

½ cup BBQ sauce of your choice

Shred left over roast (pork or beef) and place in a bowl
Add BBQsauce and mix well
Add mix into baked pie crust bottoms in pie maker
Add cheese
Place top crust
Pearce crust
Bake until golden brown
Serve with beans, potato salad or slaw
Serves 8

Roast Beef Pot Pie

A great way to use left over pot roast

Chop or shred beef

Dice vegetables

 Mix beef, vegetables and stock.

Spoon into prepared pie crust.

Place top crust

Close and bake until golden brown

Serve hot

Smoked Fish Pie

16 oz fresh haddock fillets, skinned and cut into large pieces

1 1/2 cup double cream

1 cup dry cider

7 oz large raw peeled prawns

5 oz smoked haddock fillets, skinned and cut into large pieces

2 oz frozen peas

1 oz butter

1 oz plain flour

1 large free-range egg, lightly beaten

1 bunch green onions, finely chopped

Large handful parsley, chopped

8 unbaked pastry for pie maker and tops

Melt butter in a pan. Stir in the flour and cook for a few minutes over a medium heat until it forms a thick paste.

Gradually stir in cream, until you have a smooth thick sauce.

Slowly add the cider, stirring constantly. Remove from the heat.

Stir in the prawns, both types of haddock, the peas, onions and parsley.

Spoon the mix into pie crust add top

Bake in pie maker until golden brown

Serve hot

Serves 8

Tuna Pot Pie

2 cups milk

2 cups frozen mixed vegetables, thawed

1 cup shredded Cheddar cheese

1 large can (12 ounces) tuna, drained and flaked

1/2 cup chopped onion

1/3 cup all-purpose flour

2 tsp Worcestershire sauce

1/4 cup butter

1/2 to 1 tsp salt

1/4 tsp pepper

1/4 tsp garlic and herb seasoning blend

1/4 tsp paprika

dash dried thyme, crumbled

8 mini pie crust and tops

Melt butter in saucepan

Add onion and cook over medium-low heat until tender.

Blend in flour. Add 1/2 teaspoon salt, the pepper, herb seasoning blend, paprika, and thyme.

Gradually add the milk, stirring constantly.

Cook, stirring constantly, until mixture is bubbling and thickened.

Fold in the tuna, vegetables, Worcestershire sauce, and cheese.

Taste and add more salt and seasoning if necessary.

Spoon into pastry

Place pastry tops

Bake until golden brown

Serve hot

Serves 8

Tuna Salad Pie

1 lg. can Tuna

1 can (8 oz.) tomato sauce

1/2 cup each chopped celery and pimento-stuffed olives

1 tbsp. Vinegar

1/4 cup chopped onion

1/2 tsp. Salt

Few drops of each: Worcestershire sauce and Tabasco

Dash pepper

8 baked mini pie crust

Mix tomato sauce, vinegar, and seasonings.

Chill and add celery, olives, onion and tuna.

Pour into cooled Pie Shell.

Chill thoroughly.

Serve cold

Serves 8

Turkey and Green Bean Pot Pie

4 cups Leftover Green Bean Casserole

1 cup roasted turkey meat, chopped

1/2 cup turkey, beef, or chicken stock

1/2 cup milk

8 pastry bottom and tops for pie maker

Blend leftover green bean casserole with milk, stock and turkey.

Press into bottom crust in pie maker

Fill each cup level with the top and cover with crust tops.

Cut a small hole in the top for steam. Bake until golden brown.

Repeat

Serves 8

Vegetable & Side Dish Pie

Asparagus Cheese Pie

1 pound asparagus, trimmed
8 baked mini pie crust bottoms
1 cup grated yellow cheese
1 cup grated white cheese
2 egg yolks

3 tbsp whole milk

1 tbsp minced shallot
2 tsp extra-virgin olive oil
1/2 tsp finely grated lemon zest
1/8 tsp freshly grated nutmeg
Kosher salt and freshly ground pepper

Cook asparagus until crisp but tender

Place in ice water to stop cooking

Place bottom pie crust in pie maker

Mix the cheese, shallot, egg yolks, milk, nutmeg and a pinch each of salt and pepper.

Spread mixture in pastry

Toss asparagus with the olive oil, salt, and pepper to taste and scoop into pie shells.

Bake until the cheese mixture is slightly puffy and golden.

Sprinkle with the lemon zest.

Serve warm or at room temperature.

Serves 8

Asparagus Tomato and Cheese Pie

1/2 lb. fresh asparagus
1 (8 oz.) container cottage cheese
1 (8 oz.) container sour cream
1/4 cup flour

1 egg

1 tomato, sliced
2 egg whites

5 tbsp. grated Parmesan cheese
2 tbsp. butter, melted
1/2 tsp. baking powder

Cook asparagus until tender (3 minutes).

Drain and rinse under cold water to stop cooking; drain.

Trim asparagus to fit and place in pie maker.

Place cottage cheese, sour cream, egg, egg whites, 3 tbsp Parmesan cheese into blender.

Blend for a few seconds.

Add butter, flour, baking powder and salt and mix until well blended.

Pour into pie maker over asparagus.

Bake until golden brown

Sprinkle with remaining Parmesan cheese.

Let stand for 10 minutes before serving.

Top center with thinly sliced tomato.

Serves 8

Cheese, Rice and Spinach Pie

1 10-ounce package frozen chopped spinach, thawed and
squeezed dry

3 cups cooked brown rice

1 cup diced extra-sharp Cheddar cheese

4 large eggs

1/4 cup nonfat milk

1 small onion, finely chopped

3 tbsp extra-virgin olive oil

1/2 tsp freshly ground pepper

1/4 tsp salt

3 cloves garlic, minced

Saute onions in large skillet with oil and cook, stirring frequently, until beginning to brown

Add garlic and spinach; cook, stirring, about 1 minute.

Transfer to a large bowl.

Add rice, cheese, pepper and salt to the bowl and stir to combine.

Whisk eggs and milk in a medium bowl.

Stir into the spinach-rice mixture.

Transfer to pie maker and smooth the top with a spatula.

Bake the pie until lightly browned

Let stand for 5 minutes before serving

Serves 8

Italian Style Spinach Pie

8 baked mini pie shells

16 oz. Low Fat Cottage Cheese

pkg. (10 oz.) frozen chopped spinach, thawed, well drained

1 cup shredded Mozzarella Cheese

4 eggs beaten

7 oz. Jar roasted red peppers, chopped

1/3 cup Grated Parmesan Cheese

1 tsp. dried oregano leaves

Combine ingredients and mix well

Pour into pie shells

Bake in pie maker until golden brown

Serve warm

Serves 8

This recipe works equally well as a crust-less dish

Mac and Ham Pie

3 cups shredded Cheddar cheese (12 oz)

2 ¼ cups milk

1 cup cubed cooked ham

1 cup uncooked elbow macaroni (3 1/2 oz)

2 eggs

½ cup Original Bisquick® mix

¼ tsp salt

Chopped fresh parsley, if desired

Combine 2 cups of the cheese, the ham and uncooked macaroni.

Spoon into pie maker. Saving room for biscuit mix.

Place milk and eggs in blender.

Blend on medium speed until smooth.

Add Bisquick mix and salt; blend until smooth.

Pour over mixture in pie maker.

Bake in pie maker until golden brown

Sprinkle with remaining cheese and allow cheese to melt.

Let stand 10 minutes before serving.

Sprinkle with parsley.

Serves 8

This recipe works equally well with Tuna. Tomatoes can also be added using ground beef.

Mac and Cheese Pie

8 baked mini pie crust

5 slices thick-cut bacon, cut to fit for pie tops
1 pound grated cheese

4 cups dried macaroni
2 cups heavy cream

1 egg yolk

4 Tbsp. of butter
4 Tbsp. flour
2 tsp mustard powder
Kosher salt and freshly ground black pepper

Boil pasta in generously salted water until al dente.

Cook bacon pieces in sauté pan until just crispy, drain and set aside.

Melt the butter.

Stir in the flour.

Whisk to combine and cook for 1-2 minutes.

Add cream and whisk again, let cook, whisking occasionally, until it thickens.

Whisk in egg yolk

Add mustard powder and whisk to combine.

Add all the cheese and stir to combine.

Season with salt and freshly ground pepper.

Add macaroni and cooked bacon pieces to cheese sauce, then add more freshly ground pepper to taste. Fill the baked pie crust with the mac 'n' cheese.

Place bacon slices on top and bake until done

Serves 8.

You can also use left over mac and cheese, using crumbled cooked bacon as garnish

Mushroom and Onion Pie

2 medium or large onions, coarsely chopped
1 1/2 lbs mushrooms trimmed and coarsely chopped
1/4 cup extra virgin olive oil
1/4 cup chopped fresh mint
2 large garlic cloves, minced
2 tbsp chopped parsley
1 tsp paprika
2 oz feta cheese, crumbled
Salt to taste
8 pastry crust and tops for pie maker

Heat 2 tbsp of olive oil in a large, heavy skillet over medium heat and

Add onions. Cook, stirring, until they begin to wilt, and add salt to taste.

Lower heat and cook onions, stirring from time to time, until they are very soft and beginning to caramelize.

Add mushrooms, turn the heat up to medium-high, and cook until they begin to soften.

Add garlic and stir together until fragrant, add paprika.

Cook until the mushrooms are tender and most of the liquid in the pan has evaporated.

Remove from the heat, taste and adjust salt, and stir in the mint, parsley, feta and freshly ground pepper to taste.

Brush with olive oil and place bottom crust in pie maker

Fill with the mushroom and onion mixture.

Place top crust

Pierce the top of the pie with a sharp knife.

Bake until golden brown

Mushroom Pie

1 lb diced mushrooms

2 eggs, lightly beaten

1 cup grated Monterey Jack cheese

1/2 cup cream

1/3 cup milk

1/3 cup sour cream

2 Tbsp butter1 large clove garlic, minced

A dash of ground cardamom or nutmeg (optional)

1 Tbsp chopped fresh parsley

Salt and pepper

8 mini pie crust bottoms

8 top crust disks

In a large sauté pan melt butter on medium heat. Add mushrooms, stir to coat with the butter.

Add minced garlic, stir with the mushrooms for 30 seconds and cool

Beat together the eggs, sour cream, milk, and cream.

Add freshly ground pepper, a pinch of salt, and cardamom or nutmeg.

Stir in the grated cheese and chopped parsley.

Spread the sautéed mushrooms in the bottom of the pie crust (about half full).

Pour the cheese and cream mixture on top of the mushrooms.

Place top crust

Bake until nicely browned on top and a knife inserted in the center comes out clean.

No Crust Spinach and Cheese Pie

10 oz frozen spinach, thawed and drained (spinach should be dry)

1/2 cup scallions, chopped

1/2 cup (2.5 oz) crumbled feta

1/2 cup whole wheat flour

2/3 cup fat free milk

2 large eggs, beaten

2 tbsp chopped fresh dill

2 tbsp chopped fresh parsley

2 tbsp grated Parmesan or Romano Cheese

1 tsp baking powder

1 tsp olive oil

1/2 tsp kosher salt

fresh cracked pepper to taste

Mix spinach, scallions, dill, parsley, feta cheese in a medium bowl

Sift flour and baking powder into the bowl.

Add remaining ingredients to the bowl and blend well.

Pour into pie maker.

Bake until done and repeat until all mixture is used

Let stand 5 minutes before serving

Serves 8

Portobello Mushroom Pie

4 large portobello mushroom caps
1 pear, diced

2 cups shredded cheddar cheese

6 oz salad greens (about 6 cups)

1/3 cup breadcrumbs

1 large egg, beaten
1 shallot, diced

3 tbsp extra-virgin olive oil

1 1/2 tbsp red wine vinegar

1 tsp dijon mustard
Kosher salt and freshly ground pepper
8 crust for bottom and 8 for tops

Brush the center of each pastry, tops and bottoms with mustard and season with salt and pepper.

Place the mushrooms on the pastry and season with salt and pepper.
Toss the breadcrumbs and cheese in a bowl and sprinkle over the mushrooms.

Spoon into crust

Place tops and bake until golden

Meanwhile, combine the shallot, vinegar, and salt and pepper to taste in a bowl, then whisk in the olive oil. Toss the dressing with the salad greens and pear. Serve the salad with the mushroom pies.

Serves 8

Slightly Sweet Spinach Pie

10 oz frozen spinach

4 large eggs, separated

2/3 cup granulated sugar

½ cup blanched almonds

½ cup minced candied lemon peel

¼ cup Maraschino liqueur

¼ tsp fine sea salt

Confectioners sugar for dusting

Combine spinach in a medium saucepan with salt and ¼ cup water

Cook on medium heat until water comes to a boil, cover and cook 8 minutes.

Uncover and cook 2 minutes.

Drain spinach, squeezing to press out excess liquid, then cool completely.

In food processor, pulse almonds until very finely ground; place in bowl.

Add spinach and Maraschino liqueur to food processor; purée until smooth.

In an electric mixer with paddle attachment, beat together egg yolks and ⅓ cup sugar on medium spee

Add almonds, spinach mixture and candied lemon; mix well.

In a large bowl, beat egg whites until soft peaks form.

Gradually add remaining ⅓ cup sugar; beat until whites are firm and glossy. Fold ⅓ of the eg mixture to lighten, then, in 2 additions, gently fold in remaining whites.

Immediately pour filling into pie crust.

Arrange crust tops

Bake until crust and filling are lightly golden.

Cool completely on wire rack.

Dust with confectioners sugar before serving.

Serves 8

Spicy Asparagus Pie

8 pie shell for pie maker
6 oz asparagus cut into 1-inch slices
1/2 cup blue cheese, broken into small pieces

1 cup small-curd cottage cheese
1 egg, beaten
2 green onions, diced
2 jalapeños diced and seeded
1 tbsp Tabasco sauce or salsa

Bake 8 pie shells until golden brown and remove

Cook asparagus in boiling water until crisp-tender drain and chill to stop cooking.

Combine the asparagus, cottage cheese, egg, blue cheese, onions and jalapeños.

Spoon mixture into pie shell and top with crust in pie maker.

Bake until golden brown

Serve warm

Serves 8.

Spinach and Feta Pie

2.5 lbs. spinach, chopped (fresh or frozen)

8 mini pastry crust bottoms and tops

1/2 cup olive oil

4 large onions, diced

1/2 lb. feta cheese, crumbled

1/2 lb. ricotta or cottage cheese

1/4 cup butter, melted or 1/4 cup olive oil

2 bunches green onions, diced (including green)

1/2 cup parsley, chopped

1/2 cup fresh dill, chopped or 3 tbsp. dried

1/4 tsp. ground nutmeg

4 eggs, lightly beaten

Salt and freshly ground black pepper to taste

Wash and drain the chopped spinach very well.

If using frozen spinach, thaw completely and squeeze out excess water until spinach is dry

Heat the olive oil in a deep sauce pan or large dutch oven.

Saute onions and green onions until tender.

Add the spinach, parsley, and dill and cook for 5 to 10 minutes until the spinach is wilted.

Add the nutmeg and season with salt and pepper.

Remove from heat and set the spinach aside to cool.

In a large mixing bowl, combine the feta, eggs, and ricotta (cottage) cheese.

Add the cooled spinach mixture and mix until combined.

Place melted butter or the olive oil in a bowl.

Using a pastry brush, lightly grease baked crust

Spoon mixture into crust

Place top crust

bake in pie maker until golden brown and ready to serve

Serves 8

Spinach Pie

6 lbs spinach, chopped

4 lbs feta cheese, crumbled

7 large eggs

8 mini pastry bottoms and 8 tops

2 yellow onions, diced

2 to 3 tbsp olive oil

5 bunches scallions, chopped

1 cup fresh dill, chopped

1 tsp ground nutmeg

1 tsp black pepper

1/2 tsp salt

In large pot saute onion until brown.

Add the scallions, dill, nutmeg, black pepper and salt.

Blanch chopped spinach (careful not to overcook)
Mix it together with the ingredients in the pot.

Add the crumbled feta cheese and the eggs to cooled
mixture, so the eggs don't scramble.
Bake bottom crust
Add the mix to crust and place top crust.

Bake until golden brown

Serves 8

Veggie Spinach Pie

8 cups spinach

8 baked crust for pie maker

8 tops (unbaked)

1 cup finely chopped onion

1 cup finely chopped tomato

1/4 cup lemon juice

1/4 cup olive oil

1/2 tsp salt

1/2 tsp citric acid

1/4 tsp cayenne pepper

1/4 tsp sumac

Chop and rinse spinach.

Combine spinach with 1/2 tsp salt and let sit for 15 minutes.

Drain and squeeze spinach and place in a bowl

Add next seven ingredients to spinach and combine.

Spoon mixture into baked pie crust

Top with crust and bake until golden brown

Serves 8

Vidalia Onion Cheese Pie

4 medium Vidalia onions

8 unbaked mini pie shells and tops

1/2 cup heavy cream

1/4 cup chopped ham

1/4 cup shredded cheese (any good cheese will do)

3 egg yolks and 1 whole egg

4 tbs butter

dash of nutmeg and salt

freshly ground black pepper

Dice onions

Sauté in butter until tender.

Add ham, then salt and pepper to taste

Spoon into chilled pie crust.

Sprinkle the onion mixture with shredded cheese.

Whisk together egg yolk, whole egg, and cream

Pour over the onion mixture.

Sprinkle with nutmeg

Place top crust

Bake the pie until the custard is set and the crust is browned.

Serve warm or cool.

Serves 8

Vidalia Onion Pie

3 cups Vidalia onions diced
1 1/2 cups sour cream

1/2 cup milk

4 slices bacon, crisply cooked and crumbled

3 tbsp butter, melted
8 baked mini pie shells
2 eggs, beaten

3 tbsp all-purpose flour
1 tsp kosher salt

Melt butter in sauce pan

Add the onions and sauté until lightly browned.

Place onions in pie shells

In a small bowl, beat the eggs and the flour together to combine.

Add the milk, sour cream and salt.

Mix well and pour over the onions.

Garnish with the bacon and bake until firm in the center

Serves 8

Printed in Great Britain
by Amazon

54045427R00044